100 Questions & Answers About Borderline Personality Disorder

by Laura L. Smith, PhD

for
dummies®
A Wiley Brand

100 Questions & Answers About Borderline Personality Disorder For Dummies®

Contents at a Glance

Table of Contents

Introduction

Roughly 5 million to 8 million American adults have been diagnosed with borderline personality disorder (BPD), and many more are affected by the condition, because they care about people with the diagnosis. And yet, BPD isn't part of the conversation the way other mental health conditions, like anxiety or depression or even bipolar disorder, typically are. I wrote this book to answer common questions about BPD — what it is, what causes it, how it affects the lives of people who have it, and the treatment options available.

About This Book

This book is a reference, which means you don't need to read the chapters in order from beginning to end, and you don't have to remember anything — there isn't a test at the end of it.

Within this book, you may note that some web addresses break across two lines of text. If you're reading this book in print and want to visit one of these web pages, simply key in the web address exactly as it's noted in the text, pretending as though the line break doesn't exist. If you're reading this as an e-book, you've got it easy — just click the web address to be taken directly to the web page.

Foolish Assumptions

In writing this book, I made just a couple of assumptions about you, the reader:

» You have BPD or know someone who has BPD.

» You have questions, and you want answers.

If those basic assumptions apply to you, you've come to the right place.

Icon Used in This Book

TIP

When you see the Tip icon, you'll find information that will make your life a little easier, at least when it comes to BPD.

Where to Go from Here

If you aren't sure where to begin, head to the Table of Contents and skim through the questions until you find one that catches your eye. Or, if you have a specific topic in mind, search for it in the Index. Want to know absolutely everything? Turn the page and start with Part 1.

1

Understanding Borderline Personality Disorder

This part explains what borderline personality disorder (BPD) is, what causes it, and what the risk factors are for developing it. It also walks you through the symptoms of BPD and the other conditions that may occur with BPD.

If you've recently received a diagnosis of BPD, you have a loved one recently diagnosed with the condition, or you've just met someone with BPD and you want to better understand the condition, this part is for you.

Chapter **1**

Defining Borderline Personality Disorder

How about sitting down on a blanket for a picnic lunch? At one moment, the weather is sunny and mild; then a few seconds later, the wind picks up and clouds move in. Thunder and lightning. Boom and flash! Food and plates flying everywhere! The day is ruined.

People who suffer from borderline personality disorder (BPD) may have many days like that — from calm to stormy. Like a fast-moving storm, emotions move quickly from joy to boredom or rage. Relationships with others may begin with devotion and then suddenly become fraught with conflict.

Although many people with BPD are brilliant and creative, emotional disruptions may cause their careers to be interrupted and their lives to be marked by underachievement. Impulsive behaviors complicate their already complex emotions. People with BPD have a high rate of self-harm and suicide.

Having BPD is painful, and it can be hard to love someone with BPD. This chapter gives you a glimpse at the diagnosis and definition of the disorder. I describe the process of diagnosis and offer an overview of the major signs of BPD. I also explain some of the problems with diagnosis. If you think you or someone you care about may have BPD, this chapter answers many of your questions.

What Is Personality and What Is a Personality Disorder?

You probably already have a good idea about what *personality* means. Basically, it's how someone typically acts. A person could be introverted or extroverted, open and excited by new experiences, or want everything to stay the same. They may be generally optimistic or pessimistic, dependable or unpredictable, withholding or generous.

Of course, everyone's personality can change under certain circumstances. For example, a generally contented, happy-go-lucky person may become extremely angry and aggressive when threatened. But overall, personality remains fairly stable and predictable.

A *personality disorder* is a problematic pattern of emotions, thoughts, and behaviors. Like any personality style, disorders tend to be consistent over time. People with personality disorders act very differently. For example, a small setback in life may result in unexpected rage or distress. Some people with personality disorders have little regard for the law; others are highly *narcissistic* (self-centered). Some people with personality disorders are extremely withdrawn and avoid interactions with people; others have an incredible need to be dependent and the center of attention. These patterns of behavior differ from what's expected in the culture and cause challenges in relationships, at work, and in meeting the obligations of everyday life.

What Is Borderline Personality Disorder?

BPD essentially involves a mixture of symptoms. People with BPD tend to be fragile and respond intensely to everyday challenges. Think of a delicate flower that disintegrates in the wind. There are four common features of BPD:

» **Impulsivity:** People with BPD often act without thinking about possible future consequences. They may engage in risky behaviors or self-harm.

» **Unstable mood:** For people with BPD, moods change quickly, with little provocation. They often misinterpret ordinary life as threatening or malicious.

» **Rocky relationships:** People with BPD tend to idealize others, and then demonize them, leading to multiple relationships. Their feelings may change from love to jealousy to hate.

» **Distorted thinking:** People with BPD often feel empty inside, lack direction in life, misinterpret others, and feel paranoid. They can feel dissociated from reality.

This combination of impulsivity, quick mood changes, poor relationships, and weird patterns of thinking makes BPD a difficult diagnosis to live with and to treat.

How Is Borderline Personality Disorder Diagnosed?

A licensed mental health practitioner, usually a psychologist or a psychiatrist, diagnoses BPD. The process includes a comprehensive clinical interview, which involves taking a detailed history of a person's relationships, behaviors, and moods. In addition, they'll take a complete history of previous mental health problems, emotional or physical abuse, substance use, and suicidal thoughts or acts.

Don't be surprised if a diagnosis takes more than one session. The mental health professional may wait until a strong relationship is formed so that the client is comfortable reporting all symptoms. After an evaluation comes a diagnosis and a plan for treating the symptoms.

How Do I Know if I Have Borderline Personality Disorder or Another Mental Health Condition?

Unfortunately, BPD often occurs along with other mental health issues. For example, it isn't uncommon for someone with BPD to have a substance abuse problem, depression, or anxiety. Only a qualified mental health professional can sort out those symptoms.

TIP

Although most licensed mental health professionals are able to make a diagnosis, some specialize in that area. If there is any question or doubt of a BPD diagnosis, look for a person who is experienced in working with those who have personality disorders. Call the psychology department of the nearest university for a recommendation.

Can Borderline Personality Disorder Be Misdiagnosed?

Yes, in fact, some reports show that almost 40 percent of those with a BPD diagnosis have previously been misdiagnosed. BPD shares many symptoms with other disorders.

For example, people with attention-deficit/hyperactivity disorder (ADHD) often act impulsively, but so do those with BPD. Substance abuse can lead to rocky relationships, impaired judgment, and intense emotions. Mood instability is found in those with bipolar disorder. And BPD has similar symptoms. Therefore, it's critical that people work with an experienced professional to sort out their symptoms and get the correct diagnosis.

Chapter **2**

The Causes and Risk Factors of Borderline Personality Disorder

Why do some people develop border-line personality disorder (BPD) while most people do not? Does BPD run in families? Are people with BPD abused as children? This chapter looks at all the potential causes and risk factors of BPD. Like most mental health issues, there are various reasons that seem to be related, but no one has identified a definite cause of BPD.

What Causes Borderline Personality Disorder?

When someone falls off a cliff and breaks a leg, there's not much ambiguity about what caused the break. If you're on a crowded plane and it seems that everyone around you is sneezing and coughing, and then two days later you get a cold, you likely caught that virus on the plane. If someone is pregnant, well, you can make some assumptions about what happened to cause that condition.

BPD isn't that simple. There is no known specific cause for BPD. However, after years of study and treatment, mental health professionals have some good ideas, such as genetics, trauma, and the environment.

Is Borderline Personality Disorder Inherited?

Genetics appears to be one cause of BPD. Studies indicate that in almost half of most personality disorders, the genetic makeup of an individual contributes to the development. And that's true of BPD.

Unfortunately, figuring out how much BPD is inherited is not that simple. Twins are a very convenient way to study genetic influences. Identical twins share 100 percent of their genetic makeup and, most of the time, the same environment. Fraternal twins are an effective way to consider environmental challenges — they don't have the same genes, but they do usually share the same environment.

If BPD were genetic, then if one identical twin had it, the other would, too. With fraternal twins, because they don't share all the same genes, they'd be more likely to have BPD, but the rate would be lower than with identical twins.

The problem of figuring out the exact influence is, in part, a numbers problem. If only a few percent of adults have BPD and about 3 percent of live births are twins, it's pretty hard to get a good sample of people to study who are both twins *and* have BPD.

So, it does appear that BPD runs in families, but the influence of genetics isn't clear. What we can conclude is that the inherited traits of impulsivity and unstable reactive moods (both aspects of BPD) can be inherited.

Can Trauma or Abuse Lead to Borderline Personality Disorder?

If you look back and ask someone with BPD if they suffered from physical or sexual abuse as children, the majority will answer yes. Yet a significant minority will report that they did *not* experience trauma.

Any kind of trauma is horrible. However, the type of trauma appears to heighten the risk. For example, trauma repeated over the course of years leads to more risk. Trauma (especially sexual abuse) by a family member or trusted friend appears to be worse than a single molestation by a stranger.

TIP

Interesting research looks at trauma across a wide population. Those who experience trauma are about 20 percent more likely to have significant mental illness. Surprisingly, almost 80 percent of trauma survivors go on to lead relatively normal lives, which highlights people's remarkable resilience. Protective factors include

» A supportive family
» A safe community
» Good mental health treatment after the initial trauma
» Intelligence

» A healthy personality

» Innate biological sturdiness

So, although trauma is a risk factor for BPD, it is not a cause.

How Does Childhood Affect the Development of Borderline Personality Disorder?

There is some data that says when parents invalidate or refute their children, the children are at greater risk for BPD and other mental disorders. What these parents are doing is basically saying, "You shouldn't feel that way."

Here are some examples of things parents may say that invalidate or refute their children:

» That's not true.

» What are you crying about? Toughen up!

» You're just like your father [or brother or someone else].

» Grow up and get a spine!

» That's just not right.

» You're exaggerating — it's no big deal.

» Stop thinking that way.

Chaotic families with high conflict, substance abuse, incarceration, or severe emotional disorders can harm their children, increasing the risk of future problems. These factors don't necessarily lead to BPD, but they're often reported by those who have BPD.

Are Other Risk Factors Related to Borderline Personality Disorder?

Social and cultural norms influence the way psychological pain is expressed. In some cultures, the moodiness associated with BPD isn't tolerated. Expressed anger may be very rare. Depending on where someone grows up, cutting oneself, often a symptom of BPD, would appear to be extremely odd.

The rapid changes of the world are reflected in rapid changes of behavior. Today's teens are more isolated and sheltered at home, yet they're consumers of social media with content that far exceeds their ability to understand. So, kids are more inexperienced in real life, but they're exposed to sex, violence, and aggression at younger ages online — a mixture that is sure to contribute to increasing rates of mental illness in teens and young adults.

The modern Western world encourages an open expression of feelings. If you feel angry, maybe don't hit someone, but it's perfectly okay to yell, swear, or punch a pillow. The internet allows even more violent expressions of feelings.

Can Borderline Personality Disorder Develop Later in Life?

Typically, signs and symptoms of BPD usually start in the teenage years and reach their peak in a person's 20s. An out-of-control teenager with BPD never grows up.

However, a small number of people develop BPD after the age of 30. According to the research, it appears that most people who develop BPD later share risk factors such as abuse, trauma, and even genetics. Yet they didn't show symptoms of BPD in their teens or 20s.

They had certain protective factors, such as a stable environment, fulfilling employment, higher educational attainment, or supportive relationships. Their BPD developed after some critical part of their lives fell apart. For example, they may have suffered a major loss of a loved one, a betrayal, or a critical job loss. This added stress collapsed the protective factor that kept them healthy.

Is There a Genetic Test for Borderline Personality Disorder?

At this point, there is no genetic test for BPD. Although genetic influences are likely, testing has not isolated any specific genetic pattern. It's more likely that, like many disorders, interactions between genetic vulnerabilities and the environment produce the symptoms of BPD.

TIP

The logical conclusion is that many factors contribute to the development of BPD. Future discoveries will likely reveal specific combinations that lead to BPD.

Chapter **3**

The Symptoms of Borderline Personality Disorder

Borderline personality disorder (BPD) involves mood instability, impulsivity, unstable relationships, and problems with thinking. Those broad categories can be further explored by looking at how they manifest. For example, impulsiveness may result in dangerous behaviors, gambling, drug use, or even self-harm.

This chapter takes a look at the signs and symptoms of BPD, possible patterns, triggers, and severity.

What Are the Main Symptoms of Borderline Personality Disorder?

There are nine distinct symptoms of BPD. However, a person only needs to show five of these symptoms to be diagnosed with BPD. Here are the signs to look out for:

» **Sensation seeking:** Acting, often recklessly, without thinking about the potential consequences, or just not caring

» **Self-harm:** Behaviors such as mutilating, burning, cutting, and suicidal threats or attempts

» **Extreme emotional swings:** Anger, feelings of rejection, fear, jealousy, joy, or despair, as well as strong emotional responses to perceived slights

» **Intense, inappropriate anger:** Temper tantrums, yelling, and physical fights in reaction to sometimes small, inconsequential frustrations

» **Fear of abandonment:** Fear that someone they care about may leave them

» **Unstable self-concept:** Easily threatened self-esteem; feeling competent one moment and then like a total loser the next

» **Emptiness:** Feeling lonely, bored, and empty inside; lacking a sense of purpose in life and possibly doing reckless or even dangerous activities to fill the void

» **Precarious relationships:** Falling in love intensely and putting loved ones on pedestals; feeling angry and banishing loved ones when they make one small error or cause disappointment

» **Being out of touch with reality:** Feeling outside of their own body, called *dissociation;* infrequently (for most people with BPD) experiencing paranoia, hearing voices, and having occasional visual hallucinations

What Are the Early Signs of Borderline Personality Disorder?

The first symptoms of BPD typically emerge during adolescence. Teenagers in general — not just those with BPD — are often intensely moody, get upset by small slights, act without thinking, question their own self-worth, have multiple relationships, and worry about being abandoned by their friends. And those are the very symptoms of BPD.

BPD takes normal adolescent behavior and injects it with steroids. Typically, teens outgrow their irritable, moody, impulsive behaviors, but those with BPD do not. They continue these behaviors, again on steroids, into their 20s. In addition, self-harm, thoughts of suicide, and explosiveness germinate. By early adulthood, those with BPD are usually involved in some sort of mental health treatment (from a therapist or a psychiatrist) or, sadly, in jail.

Are There Different Types of Borderline Personality Disorder?

People with BPD have different combinations of symptoms. There are nine core symptoms of BPD (for a complete list, see "What Are the Main Symptoms of Borderline Personality Disorder?" earlier in this chapter), but the diagnosis requires a person to have only five out of the nine. It's also possible to have six, seven, eight, or nine out of nine. Imagine all the possible combinations of symptoms — it's well over 200.

Based on those combinations, types of BPD include the following:

» **Impulsive:** People with this type of BPD want attention, get bored quickly, engage in risky behaviors, and/or go through multiple relationship breakups.

» **Irritable:** People with this type are pessimistic, resentful, disappointed, frustrated, and unsatisfied.

» **Dependent:** People with this type of BPD are clingy, reliant on others to fulfill their needs, worried about abandonment, and need constant reassurance.

» **Moody:** People with this type have emotions that tend to be extreme and over the top. They experience lots of mood swings and poor emotional control. They may become overly aggressive or hysterical when frustrated.

» **Self-destructive:** People with this type of BPD are harshly self-critical, engage in self-harming behaviors, have suicidal thoughts, and may attempt suicide.

What Triggers Borderline Personality Disorder Symptoms?

People with BPD are easily provoked. Certain situations cause extreme reactions. Any hint of rejection may result in fear of abandonment. That rejection can be as small as a slight delay in answering a text or being late coming home from work. Conflict also triggers BPD symptoms. Arguments, criticisms, or breakups may increase suicidal thoughts. Negative feedback from others can lead to cutting or even suicidal attempts. Memories of past traumas (real or imagined) also trigger outbursts or withdrawals.

Because people with BPD often struggle to manage their emotions, small stressors lead to big emotional responses.

How Severe Can Borderline Personality Disorder Symptoms Get?

The symptoms of BPD can be very severe, even deadly. Research indicates that people with BPD have a shortened lifespan. Some studies report a decrease of 14 to 32 years; others report a decrease of between 6 and 7 years.

Among people with BPD, the risk of suicide is higher than for those with other disorders. About 10 percent of those with BPD complete their suicide attempts. Many more have multiple attempts and experience damage from excessive cutting, substance abuse, medication abuse, or dangerous thrill-seeking behaviors.

In addition, those with BPD often have problems holding down jobs because of clashes with others, impulsive acts, or intense mood swings. They may chase away relationships that may have given them stability. Also, those with BPD often engage in unhealthy behaviors, such as smoking, substance abuse, poor diet, and lack of exercise.

TIP

The severity of BPD speaks to the need for treatment. Despite the complexity of the disorder, there are treatments that help (see Part 2 of this book).

Chapter **4**

Conditions That Occur with Borderline Personality Disorder

Often, people have a mixture of symptoms that don't quite fit a particular diagnosis. Or, even more commonly, they have more than one diagnosis. That's especially true for people who initially present with borderline personality disorder (BPD), because they often have a variety of problems at the same time. This chapter explains some of the conditions that people with BPD may also have.

How Do I Manage Borderline Personality Disorder If I Already Have Autism or Attention-Deficit/ Hyperactivity Disorder?

Autism is a disorder that is often diagnosed in childhood. People with autistic disorders have problems with social interaction. They may not understand the nuances of language and have repetitive behaviors or interests. Like autism, attention-deficit/hyperactivity disorder (ADHD) is also usually diagnosed in childhood. It manifests in lack of attention to details, impulsive behaviors, and lack of persistence. These two conditions are thought to be *neurodevelopmental* (originating during the maturation of the brain).

BPD shares a few symptoms with these two disorders. Impulsivity is a symptom of ADHD and BPD. Problems with social interaction found in people with autism are also apparent in those with BPD. Difficulties regulating emotions can be found in all three diagnostic profiles as well.

If you were diagnosed with autism or ADHD as a child and you're now being diagnosed with BPD, make sure that the health-care provider you're working with has experience working with all three disorders. Treatment may be slightly different, especially regarding symptoms that are neurodevelopmental.

How Does Borderline Personality Disorder Differ from Bipolar Disorder?

Bipolar disorder and BPD share many symptoms. People with these two conditions both suffer from mood swings. However, with BPD, moods change within a matter of moments, whereas bipolar moods usually last much longer. Also, BPD mood swings often occur after some conflict or fear of abandonment, whereas those with bipolar disorder may experience a mood swing for no apparent reason or when they experience fatigue, stress, or illness. Plus, those with bipolar disorder may have relatively stable relationships, whereas those with BPD usually have intense, unstable relationships.

It's possible to suffer from both bipolar disorder and BPD. Again, I can't emphasize strongly enough the importance of thorough evaluation and diagnosis.

Is Borderline Personality Disorder Related to Post-Traumatic Stress Disorder?

Post-traumatic stress disorder (PTSD) occurs after a perceived life-threatening or horrifying event. Symptoms include flashbacks, intrusive memories, nightmares, feeling on-guard and jumpy, and avoiding reminders of the trauma. Many people experience traumatic events, but not everyone develops the symptoms of PTSD.

Many people with BPD report traumatic events in their past, but not all do. And of those who do report trauma, not all suffer from PTSD. Therefore, trauma does not directly *cause* BPD.

TIP

If you have symptoms of PTSD, specific treatment options can be highly effective. Be sure to find a therapist with training and experience in treating PTSD.

How Does Borderline Personality Disorder Interact with Depression?

Moods generally come and go. You may feel great one day and depressed the next because it's cold and gloomy out. However, when sad moods prevail over time, you may experience a depressive disorder. Depression involves a lack of pleasure, sadness, sleep and appetite changes, as well as a general sense of pessimism that lasts more than a few weeks.

Many people with BPD suffer bouts of depression. Because those with BPD already experience a tendency to self-harm, depressive episodes should be closely monitored by a mental health professional. It's also important to distinguish between mood instability and depression. A person with BPD can appear depressed but immediately respond positively to attention and care. Those with depression can't be cheered up without treatment.

There are many successful treatments for depression, including medication, therapy, and lifestyle changes. These treatments alleviate symptoms.

How Does Borderline Personality Disorder Interact with Anxiety Disorders?

Most people with BPD have an anxiety disorder as well. Anxiety disorders include the following:

» **Generalized anxiety disorder:** People with generalized anxiety disorder worry about everything, everywhere, all the time.

» **Social anxiety disorder:** People with social anxiety disorder constantly worry about being out in social situations.

» **Panic disorder:** People with panic disorder experience intense episodes of overwhelming fear, usually accompanied by physical feelings.

» **Agoraphobia:** People with agoraphobia are afraid of leaving home, being trapped, or being in a crowd, which leads them to live highly restricted lives.

» **Specific phobias:** Intense fear of heights, snakes, bugs, animals, flying, storms, and so on are all examples of anxiety disorders.

Unfortunately, people with BPD who also have an anxiety disorder are harder to treat and have more bad outcomes than those who do not have an anxiety disorder.

Can Borderline Personality Disorder Cause Eating Disorders?

There is no known cause of BPD or eating disorders, but they do commonly occur together. Some research hints that the relationship between eating disorders and BPD is due to a problem with regulating emotions. Unhealthy eating may be an attempt to stabilize emotional responses. Impulsivity in individuals with BPD often leads to more frequent emotional eating to fill a feeling of emptiness or calm emotions.

When someone with BPD also has an eating disorder, their treatment and outcome become much more complicated. Eating disorders are serious and sometimes deadly. Both BPD and the eating disorder should be treated.

Can Borderline Personality Disorder Lead to Substance Abuse?

When stress and *emotional dysregulation* (having intense, poorly controlled emotions) are high, some people with BPD respond by using drugs and/or alcohol. Although they may be temporarily calming, overusing drugs or alcohol can lead to dependency.

Most clinicians treat substance use disorder first. But according to some research, specialized treatment for BPD can also help reduce drug and alcohol abuse.

Substance use is a factor in suicide risk. The combination of BPD impulsivity, the tendency for self-harm, and suicide attempts, along with drug or alcohol use, makes the risk of death much higher.

What If I've Been Diagnosed with Borderline Personality Disorder and Other Disorders?

Having BPD along with another diagnosis usually makes treatment more difficult, probably longer, and frankly, sometimes less likely to be successful. However, don't give up! There is much to be hopeful about.

First, find a good provider that has knowledge and experience in treating multiple disorders. Then be patient with yourself. Don't expect quick progress.

Meanwhile, find ways that you can cut down on the pressure and stress in your life. Take the time to relax, do things that give you pleasure, and understand that it will take time and effort, but you *can* expect to get better.

2

Treating Borderline Personality Disorder

IN THIS PART . . .

This part outlines where to seek help for borderline personality disorder (BPD) and the treatment options available. It dives deep into psychotherapy as a treatment for BPD, as well as medications that help with BPD.

Chapter **5**

Seeking Help

Thinking about getting professional help for borderline personality disorder (BPD)? If so, this chapter introduces you to basic questions to consider, such as when, what, where, and how.

TIP

The diagnosis and treatment of BPD and most other mental illnesses is not for the inexperienced or the untrained. Please don't rely on social media to guide your treatment.

When Should I Seek Help for Borderline Personality Disorder?

When do you go to your primary-care provider? For most people, it's maybe once a year when you get a wellness check. Otherwise, you go when you feel so sick that you can't get out of bed, go to work, or take care of your responsibilities. Most people don't go for some sniffles, but when they can't stop coughing, they see if there is something the doc can do to help.

Generally, it's the same for mental health issues. When you have feelings that keep you from doing what you need to do, like work, take care of yourself, or take care of your responsibilities, you may seek help. If you're so sad that you get no pleasure when you used to get pleasure, if you can't seem to sleep or eat normally, when life gets so overwhelming that you feel like checking out, it's time to see someone.

However, some people, especially those with personality problems, don't think they need help. They think it's the rest of the world's fault that things are going wrong. If it weren't for their ex or their boss or the economy or the neighbor or . . . you get it. They don't see their misery as their responsibility; instead, they blame others. That's why many people with BPD seek help when something happens to shake up that belief. Maybe another failed relationship, another job loss, or possibly a self-harming attempt that got too scary finally jolts them to the possibility that they may benefit from professional help.

On the other hand, some people with BPD are unhappy enough that they realize things aren't going well and it's time to seek professional care. In that case, there are many opportunities to try.

How Should I Talk to My Doctor about Borderline Personality Disorder?

You may have to start with your primary-care provider to get a referral for treatment. They may ask you to explain what's going on in your life that makes you feel like you may benefit from a mental health evaluation.

Try to describe how your daily life is impacted by your symptoms. For example, maybe unregulated emotions cause you to lose jobs or frequently lead to aggression. Maybe impulsive bursts lead to bouts of drug or alcohol abuse or dangerous behaviors. Perhaps your feelings of being unreal or unanchored have caused you considerable pain and discouragement. Or maybe you often feel like life isn't worth living and you've thought about ending your life. Make a list before you go to the doctor. Perhaps consider having a trusted friend or family member help you. Try not to get defensive or play down the negative impact these symptoms cause you.

TIP

Medical necessity refers to services suitable for evaluating, diagnosing, and treating illnesses or symptoms that affect a patient's well-being. It's often used by insurers to determine if treatment is covered.

What Should I Prepare for My First Appointment with a Mental Health Provider?

For many people, the priority when they find a provider is to determine if the provider is covered by their insurance. You can easily find out, usually online, but most insurers have toll-free phone numbers on the back of the insurance card that you can call to get that information.

After you've figured out your insurance coverage, take a few minutes to honestly look at your behaviors, thoughts, and feelings. Try to recall when they started, how uncomfortable they've become, and the impact they've had on your life. What are some of the problems that you want to change? Are you willing to accept help, even when it may sometimes feel uncomfortable?

Your provider won't be able to help you unless you're completely honest. When you see a mental health provider, they're required by law to keep the information you give to them completely confidential. There are standard exceptions to confidentiality. If you're engaged in the abuse of a child or a disabled or elderly adult, or if you're an imminent danger to yourself or someone else, then the provider must attempt to get help. Otherwise, everything you tell your provider will remain with them.

Don't be embarrassed to tell your darkest secrets. Believe me, any experienced provider has likely heard worse than what you consider shameful. Humans have a vast range of thoughts, feelings, and behaviors — some good, some bad, and some weird.

What Should I Expect During My First Appointment?

After an initial introduction and sometimes a review of confidentiality and general office policies, expect your provider to ask lots of questions. These questions may include the following:

» What brought you in today?

» How long have you been experiencing these symptoms?

» How have these symptoms impacted your everyday life?

» How serious would you rate these symptoms?

» Any other frustrations you'd like to bring up?

» Have you ever been treated for a mental health issue before?

» Have you ever experienced trauma in the past? Tell me about that.

» Who lives in your house?

- » Have you had serious relationships? Tell me about them.
- » What is your education? Did you have any trouble in school?
- » What is your job history? Any problems?
- » Are your parents alive? Is there any family history of problems like you're experiencing?
- » How do you cope with your symptoms?
- » What works best?

Most therapists weave these types of questions into a conversation that moves smoothly through the session. And some of your answers may generate new questions. By the end of the session, you can expect that the therapist will be able to tell you the next step.

What Questions Should I Ask?

During the first session, feel free to ask the therapist about their previous experience treating someone with your symptoms. Also, ask yourself if you feel comfortable with the therapist. In any helping relationship, it's important that you feel confident that you and your provider can work together.

Even though you may have already checked with your insurance provider, ask about the costs of treatment. This may also be an important time to ask about scheduling and availability.

In addition, ask about availability, office hours, what to do when you have an urgent need, and if the provider offers telehealth.

Ask your provider what type of therapy they'll provide. Is the treatment evidence-based? How long does it generally take? What does it involve?

How Do I Find the Right Treatment Option?

The next three chapters tell you about treatment options for BPD. Many factors impact which one is right for you. Some are practical — for example, are there providers near you, or is treatment covered by your insurance? Other factors include how much time you have to devote to treatment and how flexible your schedule is.

Other important issues include personal preference, comfort level, and compatibility with the provider.

What Should I Do If My Treatment Isn't Working?

First, consider that treatment for BPD takes longer than it does for other mental health problems such as depression or anxiety. That's because personality takes longer to change than mood. BPD is part of who you are as a person, so try to be patient. But at the same time, trust your instincts — if you feel that the treatment isn't for you, there's a problem. Talk it over with your therapist if you feel comfortable. If you don't feel comfortable, ask yourself why.

TIP

Those with BPD often have troubled relationships. One reason for that is because they tend to jump to conclusions about another person's intent. For example, they may feel criticized, unsupported, or angry when others are intending to be straightforward or even helpful. That goes for their relationships with therapists, too.

If you're in therapy and you become agitated by something your therapist says, talk it over with them. Try to have patience and listen to what they have to say. Don't stomp out of the office.

How Can I Advocate for Myself in the Health-Care System?

Seeking assistance can be difficult. Be prepared to advocate for yourself. First, make sure you have a good relationship with your provider. Feel free to answer questions honestly. Your provider won't be able to help you if you hide crucial information about yourself.

After you receive a diagnosis, research the diagnosis and the treatment of the disorder. Go to reliable sources such as government or university websites. Harvard Health (www.health.harvard.edu), Mayo Clinic (www.mayoclinic.org), and MedlinePlus (https://medlineplus.gov) are a few possibilities. Talk to your primary-care provider, too. If you're very concerned, ask for a second opinion.

Chapter **6**

Treatment Options

People with borderline personality disorder (BPD) have a broad array of symptoms (see Chapter 3). Those with BPD may suffer from substance abuse, job loss, relationship failures, and tumultuous emotions. The good news: There are many successful treatments. The bad news: Treatments can be long-term, difficult to access or even unavailable, and hard to complete. Nevertheless, treatments are available, and this chapter walks you through the options.

What Are the Treatment Options for Borderline Personality Disorder?

Treatment for BPD almost always includes psychotherapy, which involves a relationship between a client and a mental health provider. Within this relationship, there is a collaborative approach to problem-solving. The client and therapist work together to establish goals and a treatment plan.

Not all therapies or therapists are alike. Research studies identified the types of therapies that are most successful with people who have BPD. These types of therapies include

» Dialectical behavior therapy (DBT)

» Mentalization-based therapy (MBT)

» Cognitive behavioral therapy (CBT)

» Systems Training for Emotional Predictability and Problem Solving (STEPPS)

I cover all of these types of therapy in greater detail in Chapter 7.

TIP

A recent review of various psychotherapies indicated that most types of therapy for individuals with BPD generally improve their functioning and reduce the severity of symptoms.

Are There Any New Treatments for Borderline Personality Disorder?

A couple of new psychotherapeutic approaches are being studied. One approach, called Iconic Therapy, teaches interpersonal skills and emotional regulation. Another approach is a web-based therapy with the goal of lowering costs and improving access to care. In addition, in light of recent research indicating progress with most forms of psychotherapy, treatment by experienced therapists without specialized training is now recognized as being effective.

Scientists are also considering new biological treatments such as ketamine infusions and other new uses of medication. At this time, there is no medication approved for the treatment of BPD.

How Long Does Treatment Usually Last?

Most people with BPD are in treatment for well over a year. Indeed, it's not uncommon for therapy to be a regular part of their care over their adult years. Most people who manage to get through early adulthood have decreasing severity of symptoms beginning in their 40s.

Even after concluding treatment, people with BPD often require regular check-ins for monitoring symptoms and struggles. Having a long-standing relationship with a mental health professional gives people with BPD a stable source for problem-solving.

Can Borderline Personality Disorder Be Cured?

BPD is a chronic illness, but symptoms may come and go or be more or less severe. For example, during a period of relative stability in a relationship, someone with BPD may not engage in self-harm or feel like ending their life. But when that stable relationship ends, the same person may start cutting themselves and even attempt suicide.

Symptoms usually get better with time, especially when a person is getting treatment. Usually, impulsive behaviors and risky behaviors decrease. However, mood instability may continue even into old age. So, although an older person may not meet the criteria for diagnosing BPD (five out of nine symptoms; see Chapter 3 for more information), they may still have some residual problems related to their personality disorder.

Are There Self-Help Strategies for Managing Borderline Personality Disorder?

If you think you have BPD, you should seek help from a mental health professional. However, there is a lot you can do for yourself while getting treatment or in addition to treatment.

First, practice self-care:

» **Get enough sleep.** If you have insomnia, seek the help of a sleep specialist.

» **Exercise regularly.** Exercise helps regulate mood, improves health, and feels great!

» **Eat healthy meals.** Eating healthy foods when you're upset can be difficult, but try to have some healthy snacks around.

Stay focused on the present moment. Learn to meditate and then do it. Meditation works even with a practice of ten minutes a day (on most days). Meditation improves sleep, decreases stress, and helps memory.

Read about BPD. Find out the possible causes, symptoms, and treatments. When you find a provider, go to every session — don't cancel or reschedule. Be honest and open with your therapist — don't try to put on a show. Let them know what you're feeling, thinking, and doing.

If you decide to join an online support group for people with BPD, be careful. Some groups are great, but others are rooms to complain, be negative, and even take advantage of some members. I recommend Emotions Matter (https://emotionsmatterbpd.org), which offers resources and peer-to-peer support groups for those with BPD. Also, the National Alliance on Mental Illness (NAMI; www.nami.org) offers peer-led support groups for those with BPD and their families.

Chapter **7**

Psychotherapy for Borderline Personality Disorder

Psychotherapy helps those with borderline personality disorder (BPD). So, why don't more people get better? Part of the reason is that many people with mental illness fail to make appointments, cancel them, or quit early.

Why would people do that if therapy makes them feel better? People often find that admitting they need help is extremely difficult. And talking about feelings can be tough. A lot of people with mental illness believe that if they just tough it out, they'll feel better, and owning up to problems makes them feel weak.

If you had a sore throat that wouldn't go away, a fever, and a cough, you'd probably go to the doctor. Maybe they'd give you some antibiotics, and your symptoms would get better in a couple of days.

Mental illness is just as treatable as physical illness, but you have to participate with the provider to get better, and it takes more than a couple of days to work. *Remember:* You're the most important part of your treatment team — if you show up!

This chapter explains the role of psychotherapy in treating BPD, including different types of therapy, what to expect from a therapy session, and where to find a therapist.

How Effective Is Therapy for Borderline Personality Disorder?

Therapy is very effective at reducing the severity of the symptoms. Almost all people with BPD get better with the support of a skilled therapist. However, therapy takes time.

Although there are many types and names of therapies, those that work for BPD have some common factors:

» A positive, trusting relationship with the therapist (also known as *therapeutic alliance*)

» Primary focus on problem-solving

» Skill building in learning to deal with strong emotions

» Setting and keeping goals in therapy

» Help with understanding self and others

» Total acceptance of your emotions

» Learning to observe your own behaviors and emotions

What Types of Therapy Are Best for Borderline Personality Disorder?

Effective psychotherapies for BPD include

» **Dialectical behavior therapy (DBT):** A comprehensive approach to BPD that involves individual therapy, group therapy, and homework. Telephone support (or text support) is also available. This therapy has a heavy emphasis on emotional regulation and skills training.

» **Mentalization-based therapy (MBT):** An approach that helps people learn to interpret the thoughts, feelings, and emotions of others. This type of therapy works because people with BPD often have trouble with interpersonal relations due to misinterpreting others.

» **Cognitive behavioral therapy (CBT):** A type of therapy that helps people understand the relationship between thoughts, feelings, and behaviors. This approach is the underlying philosophy of many spin-offs, such as schema-focused therapy (SFT) and Systems Training for Emotional Predictability and Problem Solving (STEPPS). They all emphasize looking for distortions in thinking and interpreting triggering situations.

There are different names for other approaches that have limited studies to support them. They include transference-focused psychotherapy (TFP), transdiagnostic treatment, metacognitive therapy (MCT), acceptance and commitment therapy (ACT), compassion-focused therapy (CFT), and emotion-focused therapy (EFT). As long as the patient and therapist set goals, practice skills, learn better self-care, and work on interpersonal skills, these therapies are likely to improve the functioning and mental health of those with BPD.

What Is Dialectical Behavior Therapy?

DBT found its origins in CBT but has expanded to include many aspects of mindfulness-based practice. The philosophy of DBT involves *dialectics,* or the knowledge that two things can be true at once, that extremes can often lead to distortions in thinking, and that finding a middle truth is often a way to integrate both. A major dialectic in DBT is the process of full acceptance of the current state with a pull to change.

Individual therapy works on decreasing self-harming behaviors and improving willingness to change and participate in therapy. Group sessions allow clients to practice skills in emotional regulation. Homework is regularly assigned. In addition, phone consultation is available.

What Should I Expect from Therapy Sessions?

When you enter a therapist's office, either in person or virtually, you can expect lots of questions. Your therapist will want to determine your current concerns, your emotions, your struggles, your behaviors, and your thoughts.

They'll encourage you to discuss specific situations that you find troubling. Through active listening and probing questions, the therapist will help you understand what's happening, the possible causes, the consequences, and possible changes you can make.

In addition, you and the therapist should be able to specify the goals you're working on. The therapist will help you learn new ways of thinking that may impact your behavior and emotions.

How Do I Find a Therapist Who Specializes in Borderline Personality Disorder?

TIP

The *Psychology Today* website (www.psychology today.com) has a Find a Therapist feature. You can search by your city or zip code. From there, you can narrow your search by gender, as well as in person or online. You can also click All Filters to search for people who specialize in BPD, take your insurance, conduct a specific type of therapy (like CBT or DBT), and more.

If you're specifically interested in a therapist who practices DBT, check out the DBT-Linehan Board of Certification website, which has a Find a Certified Clinician page (https://dbt-lbc.org/consumers/find-a-certified-clinician). All the therapists on this site have specialized training and have passed evaluations to become certified DBT therapists. This is a highly specialized search, so depending on where you live, you may not find anyone in your local area. But if you're in a big city and overwhelmed by too many options on the *Psychology Today* website, this one can help you narrow the search.

Chapter **8**

Medication for Borderline Personality Disorder

For years, drugs called *psychotropic medications* have promised to improve emotional difficulties quickly and easily. Starting in the latter half of the 20th century, drug research continued to improve results and develop new hope for millions of people suffering from mental illness.

These drugs have been helpful for some people with borderline personality disorder (BPD), but for most people, they only reduce symptoms for a while, and many medications come with some serious or severe side effects.

This chapter covers the role of medication in treating BPD.

Can Medication Help with Borderline Personality Disorder Symptoms?

Although psychotherapy remains the best over-all treatment for BPD, medications *can* sometimes help treat specific symptoms.

Chapter 3 describes the multiple symptoms of BPD, including impulsivity, mood instability, unstable relationships, disturbances in thinking, and a tendency to harm oneself through self-mutilation, through suicide attempts, or during impulsive, dangerous behaviors. Some of these symptoms can be decreased by medication. But symptom relief does not get at the core of BPD, which is a disorder of personality. At this time, only psychotherapy appears to be able to get to these deep issues.

What Medications Are Commonly Prescribed for Borderline Personality Disorder?

The most commonly prescribed medications for BPD are *antidepressants.* Antidepressants change the chemistry in the brain. They're used to treat both anxiety and depression.

Antipsychotics are drugs usually prescribed for people who are out of touch with reality. They see or hear things that are not there and have strange, often frightening thoughts. Some research has found that these drugs have a calming effect and decrease impulsive behaviors.

Mood stabilizers are medications developed to prevent seizures for people with epilepsy. However, they also seem to smooth out moodiness and are often prescribed for people with bipolar disorder. Many people with BPD are prescribed mood stabilizers, too, although research is scant on their effectiveness. In some cases, mood stabilizers decrease emotional outbursts and impulsiveness.

Anti-anxiety medications are mild tranquilizers that are widely prescribed for everyday stress and anxiety. Unfortunately, they're highly addictive and rarely used in the treatment of BPD.

A review of multiple studies of close to 3,000 people found that medication for BPD made little or no difference in the severity of their symptoms, self-harm behavior, suicide threats and attempts, and overall functioning.

Are There Side Effects of Medications?

Many people suffer from side effects of medications, but side effects are very individual. Some people report having almost every side effect; others, none. Side effects generally get better over time. Report all side effects to your prescriber. The following are the most common:

» **Digestive problems:** These problems include nausea, constipation, and diarrhea.

» **Dizziness, often when standing up:** This condition is also known as *orthostatic hypotension,* or low blood pressure when standing.

» **Fatigue:** You may feel overwhelming fatigue even when you're getting enough sleep.

» **Sleep problems:** You may experience *insomnia* (an inability to sleep) or the opposite, sleeping too much.

» **Changes in appetite:** You may be more hungry than normal, or less hungry than normal.

» **Significant weight gain.**

» **Dry mouth.**

» **Mood swings or emotional numbness.**

» **Tremor.**

Some side effects signal danger. If you have questions, call your provider's office or poison control (800-222-1222). Tell your prescriber right away if you have the following side effects:

» **Confusion:** You don't know where you are, or you're having strange thoughts.

» **Blurry vision:** Your eyes don't seem to be working right, and things are out of focus.

» **Uncontrollable movements:** Your muscles are contracting and moving out of your control. This may include excessive blinking, tongue thrusting, hands twisting, jerking of the upper body, feet gripping, and toes extending.

How Long Do I Need to Take Medication for Borderline Personality Disorder?

Take your medication as prescribed by your provider. If you have bothersome side effects, talk with your provider. They can often help explain side effects or sometimes prescribe something else.

Never stop taking psychotropic medication abruptly on your own. You may experience increased symptoms. Your provider is likely to help you taper off slowly.

If you disagree with your provider about medication options, get a second opinion.

TIP

Can I Stop Taking Medication If I Feel Better?

Most prescribers recommend that people stay on medications for months after symptoms are gone. If you feel like you want to stop taking your medications, talk to your prescriber. They'll discuss your perceptions with you, and they may help you slowly decrease or stop your medications.

Can Medication Alone Treat Borderline Personality Disorder?

Although medications may help with BPD, they don't treat the underlying personality disorder. Psychotherapy is the only treatment with research-backed positive outcomes.

TIP

Medications are only a temporary relief from serious symptoms.

Are There Natural Alternatives to Medication for Borderline Personality Disorder?

It makes sense to lead a healthy lifestyle, including getting enough rest, eating healthfully, and exercising daily. However, no studies have found that those behaviors actually help people with BPD. At the same time, poor diet, sleep, and eating habits can induce stress, which does make symptoms worse.

Various vitamins and herbs have been suggested, such as vitamin C, vitamin D, omega-3 fatty acids, ashwagandha, valerian root, magnesium, and my favorite, chocolate. Again, actual research is very sketchy. Talk to your doctor if you want to try any of these, because some of them can impact the medication you're taking.

3

Complications of Borderline Personality Disorder

This part explains how borderline personality disorder (BPD) causes changes in thoughts and feelings, including decision-making, memory, identity, and more. It also covers the risky behaviors that people with BPD often engage in and explains why these behaviors occur.

Chapter **9**

Changes in Thinking and Feeling

Having borderline personality disorder (BPD) affects both the way you think and the way you feel. Thinking mostly involves cataloging, judging, perceiving, reflecting, predicting, relationships, and thoughts about the past and the future.

Feelings are sensations that communicate information. For example, you may feel afraid and you don't really know why, but your feeling of fear tells you to pay attention to what's around you. Feelings are not always accurate reflections of reality.

When thoughts and feelings don't match the present moment, you may misinterpret what's going on and act in inappropriate ways. This chapter answers questions about BPD thinking and feeling.

How Does Borderline Personality Disorder Affect My Decision-Making?

People with BPD often make decisions without thinking about the possible outcomes. For example, they're at a party and someone offers them a drink. They may take that drink because they believe they can stop at one. However, the past would suggest that one drink usually leads to a binge.

Another example may be when someone offers a small bit of advice or even constructive criticism. Someone with BPD may not take the advice or criticism well. They also may not remember that getting angry is rarely productive, so they react with rage. And their rage may end a relationship or a career.

Can Borderline Personality Disorder Cause Memory Problems?

Have you ever attended an event with a friend and, on the way home, you've talked about how friendly everyone was and how much fun you had, but your friend had a totally different interpretation, complaining about the coldness of the people and the horrible food? Same event, different memories. It's perfectly normal that different people have different perceptions.

However, people with BPD tend to recall more negative events and with stronger feelings than they remember positive events. In addition, people with BPD may remember things that never happened or alter their past memories.

TIP

Dissociation can also challenge the ability to remember (see "What Is Dissociation and Can Borderline Personality Disorder Cause It?" later in this chapter for more information).

How Does Borderline Personality Disorder Affect My Identity?

Identity is about all aspects of a person. For example, you may identify yourself as a binary person of color, as well as honest, hardworking, a son, a parent, an activist, good-looking, and a nuclear physicist. Throughout life, identities change; maybe you become a grandparent and a retired nuclear physicist.

When someone has BPD, their identity isn't stable, and they don't gradually change. They may feel evil or angelic. At the same time, they consider themselves devoted to their families, but they have multiple affairs, a quick temper, and a tendency to disconnect from the people around them.

Often, they change identities to mirror those of friends or lovers. BPD identities are frail and easily threatened.

What Is Dissociation and Can Borderline Personality Disorder Cause It?

Dissociation is a feeling of being disconnected. It can involve

>> Feeling out of touch with your body or mind, often looking down from above at yourself

>> Feeling the situation or environment in which you find yourself unreal, like a dream or a movie

>> Feeling totally numb and detached emotionally

>> Loss of memory of traumatic events

TIP

Dissociation is sometimes thought to be a way to protect oneself during a traumatic or overwhelming event.

BPD doesn't *cause* dissociation, but dissociation is a common *symptom* of BPD. Dissociation during interactions with others causes problems. When a person is in a state of dissociation, they may not be able to stay focused on the present reality and have trouble responding appropriately.

Does Borderline Personality Disorder Cause Emotions to Go Up and Down?

People with BPD have problems making logical decisions, difficulty remembering accurately, a tendency to perceive things as more negative than they are, an ability to step away from reality, and an identity that is fragile and easily threatened — so no wonder their emotions are like a roller coaster!

In addition, people with BPD have more and more frequent negative emotions than those without BPD. In other words, they're frequently angry, anxious, depressed, or jealous. Happiness or joy occurs much less frequently.

Plus, events that trigger negative emotions in those with BPD may seem minor to most others. For example, people with BPD can personalize the smallest hint of a slight and make it into a giant mountain of rage or despair.

Chapter **10**

Risky Behaviors

Peple with borderline personality disorder (BPD) struggle in many parts of their lives. They experience a great deal of emotional pain. After a job or relationship loss, a crisis of control, a rageful incident, or a feeling of total worthlessness, they often turn to ways to feel "less," not really better, but not in so much excruciating pain.

Self-harm behaviors in some circumstances may be a response to that deep emotional turmoil and distress. When combined with a tendency to be impulsive, those emotional Band-Aids do little to stop the flow of misery.

This chapter covers risky behaviors associated with BPD — what kinds of behaviors occur, why they happen, and what to do about them.

How Does Borderline Personality Disorder Allow Me to Act Impulsively and Engage in Risky Behaviors?

Strong urges to fill a need or desire fuel impulsiveness. For example, imagine you go into a bank and see someone take a huge withdrawal. You can't help but watch as the teller loudly counts out the $100 bills. After hitting a thousand, you start daydreaming about what a thousand dollars could buy you. Then the guy takes the money from the teller and drops it. A breeze catches the bills, and they litter the bank.

There's money all over the floor. But do you take it? Probably not. What stops you? Your brain. Although you would very much like to have some extra cash, your brain immediately checks into common sense, morality, and the likelihood of being caught, and it slams on the brakes. Your brain has a pretty good brake system.

People with BPD often have genetic predispositions to have unpredictable brain brakes. Sometimes the "brakes" work just fine. But when strong temptations arrive, these folks may not have reliable braking ability. That isn't to say they would take the money, but when other opportunities come up, they may be more prone to give in to temptation.

This impulsivity often results in risky behaviors such as drinking or using drugs to excess, having affairs, or taking risks. However, it can also result in individuals experiencing a compelling desire to engage in self-harm.

What Kinds of Self-Harm Happen with Borderline Personality Disorder?

Anywhere from 60 percent to 90 percent of people with BPD engage in *self-harm* (purposely causing injury to the body without a conscious intention to die).

Self-harming is a way some people attempt to cope with intense emotions, emotional pain, interpersonal conflict, or feelings of rejection. It can also be a way that signals their distress to others.

Common methods of self-harm include the following:

» Cutting oneself usually on parts of the body that can be hidden by clothes

» Burning one's body, often with cigarettes

» Hitting or punching (to the point of bruising, damaging walls or furniture, or even breaking bones)

- » Piercing to the extreme (not for decoration)
- » Skin picking, hair pulling, or picking at cuticles until they bleed
- » Experimenting with self-poison
- » Having intentional "accidents"

Rare self-harm behaviors include biting one's body, swallowing sharp objects, pushing one's eyeball, or inserting objects into one's body cavities.

Although people who engage in self-harm may deny suicidal thoughts or intent, the act of self-harm should be considered a warning signal that something is extremely wrong. And self-harm does increase the risk of suicide.

Professional help is needed. If you or someone you care about engages in self-harm, at least consider talking to someone at the 988 Suicide & Crisis Lifeline (https://988lifeline.org) by calling 988.

Do People Who Cut Themselves Also Want to Kill Themselves?

Self-harm may eventually predict later suicide attempts, but not always. The particular motivation of any individual can't be known, but here are some possible reasons:

- » To distract from emotional anguish
- » To replace the feeling of emptiness
- » To punish themselves
- » To get back at someone else
- » To reenact their own abuse
- » To serve as a cry for help and attention

Self-harm is dangerous, leading to disfigurement, infections, sometimes severe injuries, and even accidental death. In addition, it can escalate, causing more and more damage — potentially leading to suicide attempts.

What Is Suicidal Ideation and Is It Related to Borderline Personality Disorder?

Have you ever had a morning when the thought of getting up overwhelms you? You know what you're facing — attempting to set limits with your teenager, getting scolded by your boss, possibly a stack of bills that can't be paid, or another trip to the doctor who's likely to give you bad news. You pull the covers back over your head and wish you could sleep and never wake up. That's a mild form of suicidal ideation — but everyone feels like that way once in a while.

Simply put, suicidal ideation is having thoughts that life is not worth living, thoughts that the world would be better off without you, or thoughts that you can't take the stress, pain, hopelessness, loneliness, anger, disappointment, emptiness, and/or feelings of being trapped with no way out.

Suicidal ideation does not always end in suicide. It should serve as a warning signal that professional help is needed. About 80 percent of people with BPD have thoughts of suicide.

What Should I Do If I Have Suicidal Thoughts?

If you have suicidal thoughts, talk to someone. A professional can find appropriate treatment for you. Call the 988 Suicide & Crisis Lifeline (https://988lifeline.org) at 988. If you can't access immediate help, go to the emergency room for an evaluation.

Most people have thoughts about disappearing from a stressful time. Suicidal ideation occurs when the thought of death seems like a logical option. Others would like to die but have strong religious or spiritual beliefs, strong community or family ties, or other reasons to stay alive.

Whether your thoughts may lead to suicide or are simply a passing contemplation, suicidal ideation should be taken seriously. A mental health evaluation is crucial.

What Should I Do If I Intend to End My Life?

Stop! Get help now. Call 988 or 911 or go to an emergency room.

Suicide is a permanent solution to a problem that is likely temporary. First, promise that you won't do anything for the next 15 minutes. Then tell someone — talk to a friend or family member or call 988 to speak to a trained counselor. Take some deep breaths. Go outside and feel the air, even if it's cold, raining, snowing, or sunny. It feels real.

Make a deal that you won't do anything today. Then do something nice for yourself. Eat ice cream or chocolate. Write down what gives you pleasure in life.

Remember that thoughts come and go. Feelings come and go. They may not reflect what your life will become if you get the support you need. Take care of yourself and live.

4

Management and Lifestyle

This part is all about managing the symptoms of borderline personality disorder (BPD). It covers how to cope with and manage BPD on a daily basis, the impact BPD can have on a person's life (including work and physical health), and how to handle relationships and find social support if you have BPD.

Chapter **11**

Coping and Management

People with borderline personality disorder (BPD) struggle to control their emotions. A major focus of treatment involves techniques to manage those difficult responses. Emotional overreactions tend to be negative rather than positive. In other words, not many people complain about their intense happiness or joy. Those with BPD are challenged by feelings of emptiness, sadness, despair, anger, and rage.

Beyond therapy, which is strongly recommended, those with BPD can influence their own strong reactions with some ways to settle down. This chapter gives you some insights and ideas.

What Are the Best Ways to Manage My Symptoms?

It's hard to manage your feelings if you don't notice what you feel. To begin with, pay attention to how you're feeling. Check in with your body. Are you tense, relaxed, sad, happy, curious, or afraid? Emotions communicate how to behave. For example, anger usually requires moving toward what you're angry at. Anxiety or fear calls for avoidance or defensive actions. After you check in with your feelings, you can use your common sense and decide how to behave. For example, you may feel angry when you get that speeding ticket, but it wouldn't be a great idea to express that anger at the police officer who pulled you over.

Borderline emotions are often inaccurate reactions to reality. People with BPD may be angry and lash out seemingly without provocation. They may fear something that doesn't exist. So, try to notice your emotions and realize that you may be getting inaccurate information. Take a few deep breaths and check them out.

TIP

Emotions are always legitimate. However, they may be giving the wrong signal. Just because you feel something doesn't mean it's factual or true.

When I Feel Like Screaming in Anger, What Should I Do?

Sometimes a change in body temperature will calm you down. One technique is to take a long, hot shower or a soothing, warm bath. Another technique involves ice: Get an ice cube and hold it on your wrist. Do that until you can't stand the cold. Then take the same ice cube in the other hand and hold it on your other wrist. Keep switching wrists until the ice cube is almost melted. Check your mood. Calmed down a bit? If so, great! If not, try it again with another ice cube.

If you feel totally out of control, fill a sink or bowl with ice water and stick your face in it. Hold your breath for 15 or 20 seconds. This is especially effective for severe and intense reactions (like hysteria).

How about When I'm Losing Control of My Emotions?

Feelings communicate, but it's not always a good idea to act upon them. For example, if you get pulled over by a police officer and you start swearing and threatening them, it may end up being a poor choice.

You can't actually control your emotions, but you *can* control how you respond to them. One good technique is *doing the opposite.* For example, if you feel angry, instead of lashing out, take some deep breaths. Lower your voice. Put on a soft smile and relax your muscles. Respond softly, ask questions, but nicely. This can also be applied to depression. When most people are depressed, they don't want to do anything. Instead, take a walk, go outside, get one tiny task completed, such as loading the dishwasher or texting a friend.

People Say I Overreact — Is That Part of Borderline Personality Disorder?

People with BPD generally react emotionally to situations that may link to their core fears. The reasons are varied. Perhaps the situation left them feeling a fear of abandonment. Or maybe something that should have been a small situation became huge because of black-or-white thinking (it's either all good or all bad). It's also possible that the situation reminded them of a past trauma, which triggered a strong response.

TIP

Although it's very hard to manage, I encourage people who are relating to those with BPD to try not to take these overreactions personally. It's BPD talking, not the person.

Sometimes People Accuse Me of Being Mean or Mad, But I Don't Feel That Way — Why?

Interesting research has monitored the facial expressions of people with BPD, and the primary facial feature is disgust. Disgust is one of the main emotions of BPD. Think of seeing or smelling something rotten. Yuck, that's disgust.

Disgust helps people stay away from dangerous, possibly poisonous things. It's considered an innate response. Scientists muse that people with BPD use disgust as a defensive technique for staying away from any possible threat. Unfortunately, it contributes to interpersonal problems when others are attempting to communicate.

How Do I Explain Borderline Personality Disorder to My Family and Friends?

Don't tell everyone you know about your diagnosis. Evaluate the necessity of giving them that sort of personal information. With close adult family members, you may want to discuss some of the symptoms and problems that you're experiencing. Talk to your therapist for some suggestions.

Understanding your diagnosis may help your family be more supportive and less personally upset. For young children, little is probably better. For older children, you may tell them about your difficulties in controlling your emotions. Be sure to let them know that you're working on making that better.

TIP

You may want to discuss your diagnosis with a close friend, but I wouldn't make it a frequent topic of conversation. Acknowledging that you have problems with emotional regulation and interpreting social nuances may result in their giving you more grace.

What Should I Do If I'm Having a Crisis?

A *mental health crisis* is when you feel that you're in imminent danger of hurting yourself or someone else. In that case, you need immediate emergency care. Call 911 or go to an emergency room. Staffed by dispatchers, 911 will send out rescue personnel such as police, fire, or ambulance.

If your situation doesn't involve immediate danger, call 988. (Veterans can get specialized care by dialing 988 and pressing 1.) If your doctor has an on-call availability, call them. Calling 988 connects you with a specially trained person who will help you get through the crisis, notify emergency personnel, or problem-solve with you to get the help you need.

If you're experiencing a crisis and you think you can calm yourself down with the help of a trusted family member or friend, call them. However, if they're hesitant, afraid, or not available, 988 will get you the help you need.

Are There Support Groups for People with Borderline Personality Disorder?

If you're able to receive dialectical behavior therapy (DBT; see Chapter 7), there is a group component in the treatment. The National Alliance on Mental Illness (NAMI) also has support groups (usually online).

Be wary of social media support groups — they can become very negative and invasive. Talk to your healthcare provider about other sources of support in your area. If you receive therapy from a specialist in BPD, they can suggest other ways to get additional support.

What Are Some Lifestyle Changes I Can Make to Manage My Borderline Personality Disorder?

The best way to manage BPD is to get evidence-based psychotherapy. Next, make sure that you're living a healthy lifestyle — eat a healthy diet, get enough sleep, and try to exercise on most days.

TIP

While you're in treatment, try to reduce stress in your life as much as you can. Don't volunteer for extra projects at work, take on a foster child, or dump an important relationship. Try not to make important decisions in your life until you've experienced treatment. If you must make major changes, talk to your therapist to help you figure out options.

I Feel Better — How Can I Prevent a Relapse?

With psychotherapy, most people with BPD can expect to get better. Also, with age, some BPD symptoms are likely to decrease. Think of BPD like having a learning disability in emotional control and interpersonal skills.

You need clear learning strategies, practice, and repetition to master these skills — and that takes time. Don't rush through therapy. Try to have a therapist available for checkups or extra support when you need it.

TIP

Stay away from toxic people, find work, and be healthy. Keep doing what you've been doing to be better, and expect a relapse here and there. Overall, you can expect a normal life.

Chapter **12**

Impact on Life

Borderline personality disorder (BPD) shows up in a variety of ways, including unstable relationships, unregulated emotions, dangerous behaviors, impulsive actions, and confusing thoughts. This chapter looks at how these symptoms impact the lives of those with BPD.

How Does Borderline Personality Disorder Affect Day-to-Day Life?

Everyday life is full of obstacles for someone who suffers from BPD. For example, a frustration that may seem minor, such as someone showing up late for lunch may have huge emotional consequences for those with BPD. They may feel personally insulted by the lateness and get angry, or they may believe that their lunch date is abandoning them, so they feel despair and pain.

Someone who is pretty well adjusted would likely wonder if traffic or something else caused the lateness. Perhaps, they may be a bit annoyed, but they're unlikely to have a huge emotional response.

Can I Have a Successful Career with Borderline Personality Disorder?

Some people with BPD are hugely successful. However, many have multiple problems keeping a steady job. Almost half are either unemployed or eligible for disability. BPD is a serious illness that affects multiple aspects of a person's ability to keep and hold a job.

For example, they may relate to coworkers in an inappropriate way, either idolizing or demonizing them. They may have emotional outbursts, become moody or depressed, or even appear to check out of the present moment.

Some workers with BPD have problems with absenteeism or tardiness due to their emotional distress; others lose interest in a job when the demands of the job become emotionally overwhelming.

How Does Borderline Personality Disorder Affect Relationships?

Relationships are a struggle for people with BPD. There are often cycles of love and kindness, followed by breakups, and then passionate reunions. The black-and-white thinking of someone with BPD can mean that they see their partner as either all good or all bad. The shift between these extremes can stem from a minor incident, like folding the laundry the wrong way or forgetting to get the mail.

People with BPD have trouble understanding the needs, feelings, and beliefs of others. They have difficulty walking in someone else's shoes and seeing their perceptions. When strong emotions overwhelm those with BPD, it's almost impossible for them to look outside of their own intense emotional experience.

Can Borderline Personality Disorder Affect My Physical Health?

People with BPD tend to die younger than those without. In fact, many studies suggest that lifespans are about 20 years less. One in ten people with BPD commits suicide. People with serious mental disease, including those with BPD, are more likely to smoke cigarettes, shortening their lives.

Furthermore, those with BPD tend to over-indulge in drinking and drug use. Accidental deaths, such as traffic accidents or drug over-doses, are more common. Poor nutrition, lack of exercise, and poor sleep also lead to shorter lifespans.

TIP

Before working on significant lifestyle changes, it's important to get treatment for BPD. That's because without changes in thinking, lifestyle changes are more likely to be transient.

How Does Borderline Personality Disorder Affect My Self-Esteem?

To understand what BPD does to self-esteem, first, you must understand the concept. Self-esteem involves three components:

» A perception or observation of some quality of yourself

» An evaluation of that quality

» An emotional response to that quality

Say you play softball on Saturday nights with some friends. Are you a good player? Well, you strike out almost every time, you can hardly catch the ball, and you're incredibly slow getting to first base. So . . . probably not. However, you primarily play because your friends are all playing for fun. They don't care if they win or lose — it's the food and drink after the game that you and everyone on your team plays for. So, you're a bad softball player, but it doesn't upset you.

Let's say you have BPD. This same situation may set off a flood of overwhelming shame. Losing at any game or situation is soul-shattering. You think you're a worthless person.

People with BPD tend to have fragile egos that shatter easily. That's what BPD does to self-esteem.

Does Borderline Personality Disorder Prevent Me from Being a Good Parent?

BPD does not prevent you from being a good parent. First, if you're in treatment, talk to your therapist about any struggles you may have with being a parent. Many very successful parent training programs are available. Take one.

You probably have difficulty controlling your emotions. Talk to your therapist if you have outbursts with your child. Develop a support system. Make sure your child has another place to go when necessary and a person to talk to. If you feel overwhelmed, allow others close to your child to help out.

You'll do your best as a parent if you have time to be alone. During that time, breathe, reflect on your role, and realize that you're doing the best you can.

How Does Borderline Personality Disorder Affect My Social Life?

One of the most difficult symptoms of BPD is unstable relationships. Working with a psychotherapist can help you learn better interpersonal skills that allow you to establish relationships.

Take care to seek relationships that won't exaggerate your BPD symptoms. For example, it's probably not a good idea to hang out at a bar. Getting drunk or high in general is more likely to lead to risky, dangerous behaviors.

Try to fill your relationship needs with supportive family and friends.

Can Borderline Personality Disorder Affect My Academic Performance?

BPD can make going to school more challenging. Most people with BPD have the ability to continue their education after high school.

However, problems with concentration and attention may occur. Feeling personally threatened by other teachers or students can lead to emotional outbursts. Collaboration with others can be challenged by poor interpersonal skills.

People with BPD also tend to be impulsive and driven to exciting activities. Usually, school requires quiet effort and study, which may be hard for someone driven to excitement.

TIP

Here are some strategies that may improve academic achievement for someone with BPD:

>> Find a good tutor to help structure time, support good study habits, and set realistic goals.

>> Keep a calendar of all activities and goals.

>> Continue psychotherapy to encourage skill building.

>> Open communication with teachers and support staff.

>> Set a realistic schedule with downtime.

>> Continue to lead a healthy lifestyle.

Chapter **13**

Relationships and Social Support

Good relationships with people predict better mental and physical health. Those with good relationships tend to live longer and suffer less cognitive decline as they age.

People with borderline personality disorder (BPD), by definition, usually have tumultuous relationships. Their relationships are often full of arguments, chaos, and eventually breakups. However, there is hope. With treatment and learning new skills, those with BPD can become better friends, partners, and neighbors.

This chapter is all about relationships — how to have healthy ones, what to tell your partner about your condition, how to set boundaries, and more.

How Can I Build Healthy Relationships If I Have Borderline Personality Disorder?

All people have thoughts, feelings, opinions, and emotions. A skill that many people, especially those with BPD, lack is the ability to put themselves in others' shoes. In other words, they have trouble understanding that they have different thoughts, feelings, opinions, and emotions. People with BPD often think that everyone thinks and feels as they do — and if they don't, then they're absolutely wrong. Taking another perspective involves a conscious awareness of other people and considering what they may be feeling or thinking. Therapy helps people with BPD learn to be better at understanding that other people have different thoughts and feelings.

People with BPD often use projection as a way to protect themselves from discomfort. *Projection* occurs when someone takes their own painful, negative feelings and attributes them to someone else. For example, if you feel angry, you deny your anger and say someone else is angry.

It's a way of *not* dealing with your own distress. If you have a poor body image, then you may spend lots of time criticizing others' bodies.

You can decrease projection by increasing your own self-awareness. Try to be honest with yourself about how you're feeling and thinking.

What Should I Tell My Partner about My Borderline Personality Disorder?

If you're in a serious relationship, your partner probably knows that something is different about the way you feel, think, and behave. Telling them about your diagnosis should be done in a quiet setting. Allow time to answer questions and process. Some people like to have their partner come to a therapy session to help with understanding and processing.

If you decide to share your diagnosis with your partner, be informed about your symptoms, possible causes, and how you sometimes act out. Also, give them the hopeful news about the success of the treatment. It may be a good idea to apologize if your BPD symptoms have caused your partner distress. Expect lots of questions, and keep your emotions calm.

How Can My Family Support Me with My Borderline Personality Disorder?

Your family can be your biggest support. They can provide unconditional love and acceptance. They can forgive and understand your struggles. However, when you have a supportive family, you have an obligation to get treatment. Don't forget that BPD is highly and usually successfully treatable. Your family can become your very own cheer team.

Also, realize that those closest to you are often the ones who take the brunt of your emotional outbursts. Make sure that you show and tell them how much they mean to you and how much their support helps. "I'm sorry I hurt you," and "I love you," are wonderful Band-Aids to emotional pain.

How Can I Handle Conflicts in Relationships If I Have Borderline Personality Disorder?

People with BPD are easily provoked and often make assumptions about the intentions of other people. Those assumptions suppose that the intention was malicious. A simple statement from someone such as "Did you pick up the mail on your way home?" may be construed as "He's calling me lazy and forgetful," instead of being curious about the mail. For people with BPD, having malicious assumptions often begins a conflict when none existed before.

If there is a conflict, take a few deep breaths. Delay responding for at least 15 seconds. Look for malicious or incorrect assumptions. Most conflicts are over minor things, so let them go.

How Can Borderline Personality Disorder Affect My Friendships?

Lots of people with BPD have close friendships. However, BPD can spell trouble in certain situations. BPD enthusiasm may encourage you to attempt to get too close too soon. For example, it's usually not a good idea to disclose detailed personal information upon meeting a person for the first time.

You may feel like your friend is the best person around and flatter them too much. This could make them cautious and cause them to back away from you.

Another problem is wanting to spend too much time with a friend. Most people have multiple obligations and may not want to immediately start seeing someone frequently. Resist the desire to keep in constant contact.

Finally, BPD relationships often end in conflict. When your friend inevitably disappoints you, try not to be too critical. They're human and make mistakes, too.

How Can I Set Boundaries in Relationships If I Have Borderline Personality Disorder?

If you have BPD, you may find that you're easily triggered. Boundaries can help you navigate and hopefully keep you from becoming overly emotional.

First, think about your own values. How do you want others to treat you? How would you like to handle conflict? How much time alone do you need? Do you need your own space to retreat to?

When you've identified your own values, express yourself calmly using *I* statements. Here are some examples of *you* statements versus *I* statements:

You Statement	*I* Statement
You're always late, and you never text to tell me where you are.	I feel scared and worried when you're late and don't text.
All you do is yell.	I can't understand what you're saying when you raise your voice.

You Statement	*I* Statement
You never remember to take out the trash.	I would really appreciate it if you could help around the house by taking out the trash without needing a reminder.
You hate my parents.	I know my parents can be a lot, but I love them and I would love it if you could try to get along with them.

Remain calm and take deep breaths when you feel agitated. Conflicts are best resolved when boundaries are enforced. Seek help from your therapist about other ways you can set appropriate boundaries with others.

What Role Does Social Support Play in Managing Borderline Personality Disorder?

Social support or having a group of people who can help you, spend time with you, and be there when you need an extra hug are critical to healing. Those with BPD need a few people who accept them and care about them regardless of their behavior. Supporters can disapprove of your behaviors, but still accept you as a worthy person.

Interesting research indicates that for those with BPD, *perceived social support* — that is, believing they have support — is actually more important to well-being than actual social support. That means if people with BPD believe they have supportive people in their lives, that's enough.

How Can I Improve My Communications with Friends and Family?

Problems with communication are particularly common in people with BPD. For example, there is often a communication style that begins with the person with BPD starting to talk, primarily about themselves. This monologue goes on and on. There appears to be very little interest in the other person's opinions or responses. This causes the listener to emotionally disconnect. So, what starts as *expression* by one person leads to *disconnection* by the other and finally *rejection*.

Most people know someone who has that communication style. The expressive person goes on and on without showing any interest in you, the listener. When that happens, it's only natural to disconnect and, finally, if the pattern continues, reject or avoid the person who doesn't know how to have a conversation.

TIP

It takes two to tango or communicate. If you find yourself talking more than half of the time, ask yourself why.

5

Living with Borderline Personality Disorder

This part is about living with borderline personality disorder (BPD). It discusses the prognosis and long-term outcome for people with BPD and ends with a focus on self-understanding and personal growth, including the impact of meditation, diet, exercise, and more.

Chapter **14**

Prognosis and Long-Term Outcome

The treatment of borderline personality disorder (BPD) has made great progress over the last few decades. Life with BPD is no longer considered a dangerous dance from crisis to crisis. Today, people with BPD who are able to get adequate treatment can look forward to seeing much improvement. However, the big problem is keeping focused and staying in treatment long enough for therapy to be effective. This chapter addresses prognosis and continuing and cooperating with the treatment plan.

How Can I Stay Motivated during Treatment?

The goal is to feel better — keep that long-term goal in mind. That's how to stay motivated. People usually don't go to therapy unless their lives are unsatisfying, they feel bad, or they get into lots of trouble.

Those with BPD often have trouble with relationships, jobs, mental anguish, and reckless behaviors. There is every reason in the world that they want to feel better.

How Can I Track My Progress throughout My Treatment?

One great way to keep track of progress is by keeping a daily journal. It doesn't have to be poetic — just keep track of your moods, your daily activities, and your relationships. Add a bit of good self-care by noting something that you're grateful for that day — gratitude improves mood.

Progress in therapy almost always resembles the stock market: It fluctuates from high to low. Sometimes the low times look bleak and last too long, but generally, over time, the stock market goes up. Therapy is like that, too. Gradual gains, with some short periods of readjustment. Be patient.

What Are the Overall Success Rates of Various Treatments for Borderline Personality Disorder?

There is very good news about treatment success rates. A significant number of people, over time, get better. Most of those with treatment report being in remission after several years.

The other good news is that most psychological treatments are successful. Prior to this new research, it was thought that the best success could be achieved in a treatment known as dialectical behavior therapy (DBT), which required participation in individual therapy as well as group therapy. Many locations, especially rural areas, didn't have access to DBT. But today, treatment can be offered by trained mental health therapists without the specialized method that is required for DBT. Many therapists use the techniques of DBT without the full method.

What Is the Long-Term Outlook for People with Borderline Personality Disorder?

People with BPD who receive treatment can look forward to a decrease in symptoms over a few years. However, there is consensus that treatment should be available for flare-ups or relapses. Generally, those with a stable partner and occupation do better than those who are physically or mentally disabled or without a partner.

Do All Borderline Personality Disorder Symptoms Improve with Age?

It appears that impulsivity and self-harm behaviors improve over time. However, feelings of emptiness and fear of abandonment tend to remain more difficult to treat.

Many therapists feel that if they can keep their clients alive through their twenties, the person is less likely to die by suicide. However, the risk of committing suicide in their 30s remains high. As many as 10 percent of those with BPD are successful at ending their lives through suicide.

Can People with Borderline Personality Disorder Live Normal Lives?

One of the many predictors of a better outcome for all people with mental illness is having meaning and purpose in their lives. Either an occupation or volunteer work can keep people busy and give them meaning and purpose. Those activities improve the overall functioning of people as they navigate BPD. Spending more time and effort on vocational rehabilitation, along with therapy, may make sense. Sitting at home on social media, playing video games, or engaging in other passive pursuits are not helpful pastimes.

Having a supportive partner or friend helps maintain stability and a normal life. Although it takes work, people with BPD can make slow and steady progress.

Chapter **15**

Self-Understanding and Personal Growth

When you're sleep deprived, stressed out about your job, not feeling well, or overwhelmed, it's easy to feel defeated. This chapter is about decreasing stress and handling difficult emotions.

Stress increases blood pressure, interferes with sleep, makes us forgetful, contributes to heart disease, upsets the digestive system, and impairs the immune system. It can also cause chronic pain because of tight muscles.

Everyone gets stressed, but people with borderline personality disorder (BPD) have even more stress. That's because they often have conflict in their lives, as well as feelings of fear, unworthiness, and emptiness. Managing stress and increasing resilience are critical parts of coping with BPD.

What Resources Are Available for Me to Better Understand Borderline Personality Disorder?

First, find out as much as you can about BPD. Reputable health resources such as WebMD (www.webmd.com), Healthline (www.healthline.com), and Mayo Clinic (www.mayoclinic.org/diseases-conditions) have information about BPD and other disorders. Check your sources and don't rely simply on social media for accurate data. And don't get a diagnosis from an online quiz.

A second source of material about BPD should be your psychotherapist. BPD is a complicated problem, and your symptoms are unique to you. Your therapist knows you and how to best communicate with you.

Finally, you can turn to your trusted source, the *For Dummies* series. Check out *Borderline Personality For Dummies,* 2nd Edition, by Charles H. Elliott and I, as well as *DBT For Dummies* by Gillian Galen and Blaise Aguirre (both published by John Wiley & Sons).

What Role Does Mindfulness Play in Managing Borderline Personality Disorder?

Mindfulness practice involves nonjudgmental awareness of the present moment. The key word is *nonjudgmental.* That means a complete acceptance of what is here and now.

Mindfulness often involves the practice of meditation. Although there are many different kinds of meditation, most include focused breathing and attention.

A practice of mindfulness for people with BPD helps them regulate strong emotions and gives them the skill to become good observers of reality.

Does Sleep or Diet Affect Borderline Personality Disorder Symptoms?

The life expectancy of people with BPD is strikingly lower than for those with other mental health problems. Although suicide is one factor, another is an unhealthy lifestyle. People with BPD often engage in risky behaviors, such as smoking, drinking, or drug use. They may drive recklessly, have eating disorders, and have poor sleep habits. Those activities add to the huge burden of having BPD.

It's crucial to live a healthy lifestyle to combat the risks of BPD. Adequate, regular sleep and a good diet are parts of a commitment to good health. And most importantly, don't stress out if you aren't perfect. You don't need to be more stressed — just do the best you can!

What Role Does Exercise Play in Addressing Borderline Personality Disorder?

Exercise lowers the risk of just about everything that stress does to your body. It also improves your mood. There are four major types of exercise:

» **Endurance:** Also known as cardio, endurance work helps the heart and brain stay healthy. Adults should get about two and a half hours per week.

» **Strength training:** Lifting weights keeps bones and muscles strong. Start with small weights and gradually build up. Do this at least two times a week.

» **Flexibility:** Stretching before and after other exercises improves flexibility.

» **Balance:** Balance work decreases risks for trips and falls. It also helps with core muscles.

How Can I Develop Self-Compassion If I Have Borderline Personality Disorder?

Understanding that BPD is not something that you chose is the first step to developing self-compassion. Just as mindfulness encourages acceptance and nonjudgment of the present moment, you can develop self-compassion.

Affirmations often begin a self-compassion practice. Be sure to pick a few or make them up yourself. Affirmations should be personal and resonate with what you're working on. Here are some examples:

» I am a worthwhile person.
» I forgive myself when I get lost.

- » I can learn new things.
- » I deserve a good and happy life.
- » My challenges are difficult, but I'm handling them.
- » I did the best I could today.
- » I accept who I am.

How Can I Build Resilience with Borderline Personality Disorder?

As you move through your treatment for BPD, acknowledge to yourself that, with time and work, you will get better. Imagine your future life. You don't want to be sitting at home scrolling through social media or playing video games. Although those can be amusing activities, people in recovery do better with activities that provide meaning and purpose.

Consider what you would do if you were feeling good, not struggling with emotional outbursts, confident, and able to have easygoing relationships with people. Decide now on some steps to build resilience. Taking a job (either part-time or full-time), going back to school, getting more training, or volunteering are good activities for recovery.

Part of resilience is also a healthy lifestyle, which includes diet, sleep, and exercise. Also, think about making meditation a regular part of your day.

Why Should I Feel Grateful If I Have Borderline Personality Disorder?

At first glance, that question may seem silly. Why should you be grateful for BPD? Overall, BPD makes people miserable. But here are a few reasons you may be a better person because of your BPD:

» BPD has made you bold and able to speak up for yourself.

» Through your struggles, you've become more resilient.

» You study people. Sometimes you misinterpret, but with skill and practice your intuition is already highly developed.

» Many people with BPD are highly intelligent and creative.

» Your intense emotions make you passionate and loving.

The intensity of emotions of BPD includes wonderful highs, as well as desperate lows. What makes people with BPD weak also makes them strong. With treatment, those painful symptoms become personal strengths.

Index

individual therapy, 53

insurance
  coverage, 38
  provider, 40

intense, inappropriate anger and BPD, 20

interpersonal skills, 45, 95

intrusive memories, PTSD, 28

irritable BPD, 22

J

jealous, 69–70

job, 24, 108
  loss and BPD, 43

joy, 69–70

judging, 65

K

ketamine infusions, 45

kindness, 91

L

lack of exercise, 24

life expectancy, 116

lifestyle, 61
  changes, 87
  unhealthy, 116

love, 91, 100

M

magnesium, 61

management, 115
  stress, 114

Mayo Clinic, 42, 114

medical necessity, 38

medication
  abuse, 24
  duration, 59–60
  efficiency, 56
  natural alternatives, 61
  psychotropic, 55
  side effects, 58–59
  when to stop, 60
  withdrawal/stopping, 60

meditation, 47

MedlinePlus, 42

memories of past traumas and BPD, 23

memory problems, 67

mental anguish, 108

mental health, 97
  crisis, 86

mental illness, 50

mentalization-based therapy (MBT), 44, 51

metacognitive therapy (MCT), 52

mindfulness, 115

About the Author

Laura L. Smith, PhD, is an author and a clinical psychologist. She is a past president of the New Mexico Psychological Association. Laura has worked in private practice, within hospital settings, and as a consultant for schools. She has presented workshops on cognitive therapy and mental health issues to national and international audiences.

Laura is the author *of Narcissism For Dummies; Anxiety & Depression Workbook For Dummies,* 2nd Edition; *Obsessive Compulsive Disorder For Dummies,* 2nd Edition; and *Anger Management For Dummies,* 3rd Edition (all published by Wiley). She is coauthor with her late husband, Dr. Charles Elliott, of *Quitting Smoking & Vaping For Dummies; Borderline Personality Disorder For Dummies,* 2nd Edition; *Child Psychology & Development For Dummies; Seasonal Affective Disorder For Dummies;* and *Depression For Dummies,* 2nd Edition (all published by Wiley).

Dedication

I dedicate this book to my extended family and friends who surrounded me with love and caring throughout this difficult time. And to the voice who will always be in my head and in my writing, Charles Elliott.

Publisher's Acknowledgments

Senior Managing Editor:
Kristie Pyles

Associate Editor:
Elizabeth Stilwell

Editor: Elizabeth Kuball

Production Editor:
Magesh Elangovan

Cover Design and Image:
Wiley

Special Help:
Carmen Krikorian

Printed and bound by CPI Group (UK) Ltd, Croydon, CR0 4YY

14/07/2025

14702804-0001